Book and CD for B♭, E♭, C and Bass Clef Instruments

Arranged and Produced by
Mark Taylor and Jim Roberts

CD BOOK

TITLE	PAGE NUMBERS			
	C Treble Instruments	B♭ Instruments	E♭ Instruments	C Bass Instruments
Bridge over Troubled Water	4	24	44	64
Cecilia	6	26	46	66
El Condor Pasa (If I Could)	8	28	48	68
The 59th Street Bridge Song (Feelin' Groovy)	10	30	50	70
Fifty Ways to Leave Your Lover	12	32	52	72
Homeward Bound	14	34	54	74
Loves Me Like a Rock	16	36	56	76
Mrs. Robinson	18	38	58	78
Slip Slidin' Away	20	40	60	80
Still Crazy After All These Years	22	42	62	82

TITLE	CD Track Number Split Track/Melody	CD Track Number Full Stereo Track
Bridge over Troubled Water	1	2
Cecilia	3	4
El Condor Pasa (If I Could)	5	6
The 59th Street Bridge Song (Feelin' Groovy)	7	8
Fifty Ways to Leave Your Lover	9	10
Homeward Bound	11	12
Loves Me Like a Rock	13	14
Mrs. Robinson	15	16
Slip Slidin' Away	17	18
Still Crazy After All These Years	19	20
B♭ Tuning Notes		21

Cover photo © Retna

ISBN 978-1-4234-8923-8

Music Sales America

Visit Hal Leonard Online at
www.halleonard.com

PAUL SIMON

Volume 122

Arranged and Produced by
Mark Taylor and Jim Roberts

Featured Players:

Graham Breedlove–Trumpet
John Desalme–Saxes
Tony Nalker–Piano
Jim Roberts–Bass
Todd Harrison–Drums

Recorded at Bias Studios, Springfield, Virginia
Bob Dawson, Engineer

HOW TO USE THE CD:

Each song has two tracks:

1) Split Track/Melody

Woodwind, Brass, Keyboard, and **Mallet Players** can use this track as a learning tool for melody style and inflection.

Bass Players can learn and perform with this track – remove the recorded bass track by turning down the volume on the LEFT channel.

Keyboard and **Guitar Players** can learn and perform with this track – remove the recorded piano part by turning down the volume on the RIGHT channel.

2) Full Stereo Track

Soloists or **Groups** can learn and perform with this accompaniment track with the RHYTHM SECTION only.

CD

BRIDGE OVER TROUBLED WATER

WORDS AND MUSIC BY
PAUL SIMON

C VERSION

Fmi7/Bb Ebma7 /D
Eb7/Db Bbmi6 A+7 Abma7 A+7 Bbmi7 Eb7 /G
Abma7 Bb/Ab Gmi7 Cmi7 /Bb Abma7 G+7(b9)
Cmi7 Bbmi6 A+7 Abma7 Bb/Ab Gmi7 Cmi7
Fmi7 Fmi7/Bb Ebma7 Db6
LAST X ONLY
Ebma7 Db6 D6 Ebma7
Db6 Ebma7 Abma7
Ebma7 Dmi7 Cmi7 Fmi7/Bb
Ebma7 /D Eb7/Db Bbmi6 A+7
Abma7 A+7 Bbmi7 Eb7 /G Abma7 Bb/Ab
Gmi7 Cmi7 /Bb Abma7 G7(b9) Cmi7 Bbmi6 Eb7
Ab6 Abma7 Bb/Ab G+7(b9) Cmi7 Fmi7 Fmi7/Bb
Db6 Fmi7/Bb F/Eb

CD

C VERSION

CECILIA

WORDS AND MUSIC BY
PAUL SIMON

N.C./F
F7ADD4
F7
PIANO
E♭/F
F7
D.S. AL CODA
CODA
F7ADD4
F7
E♭7/F
F7
F7ADD4
F7
E♭7/F
F7

C VERSION

EL CONDOR PASA

(IF I COULD)

ENGLISH LYRIC BY PAUL SIMON
MUSICAL ARRANGEMENT BY JORGE MILCHBERG
AND DANIEL ROBLES

SOLO
Cmi7 F7 Cmi7 F7 Cmi7 F7 Cmi7 F7
Cmi7 F7 Cmi7 F7 Cmi7 F7 Cmi7 Cmi7/Bb
Abma7 Ebma7 A7
Abma7 Gmi7 Fmi7 Ebma7 G+7(#9)
Cmi7 F7 Cmi7 F7 Cmi7 F7 Cmi7 F7
Cmi7 F7 Cmi7 F7 Cmi7 F7 /Eb Db7(b5)
D.S. AL CODA
CODA
Db7(b5) Cmi6

CD

C VERSION

THE 59TH STREET BRIDGE SONG

(FEELIN' GROOVY)

WORDS AND MUSIC BY
PAUL SIMON

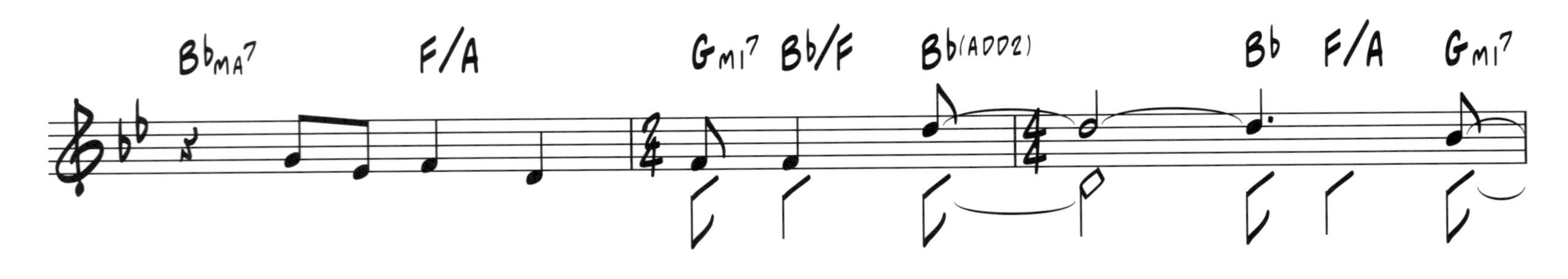

4.
Gmi7/C C/Bb F/A G6 Fma7 C/E Bb/D Cma7
Bb(add2) Ami7 Gmi7 F(add2) Eb(add2) Dmi7 Cma7 G/B
Ami7 C/G C(add2) C G/B Ami7 G/B C(add2)
C G/B Ami7 F/A G6 Fma7 C/E
Bb/D Cma7 Bb(add2) Ami7 Gmi7 F(add2) Eb(add2) Dmi7
Cma7 G/B Ami7 C/G C(add2) C G/B Ami7
G/B C(add2) C G/B Ami7

CD

FIFTY WAYS TO LEAVE YOUR LOVER

WORDS AND MUSIC BY
PAUL SIMON

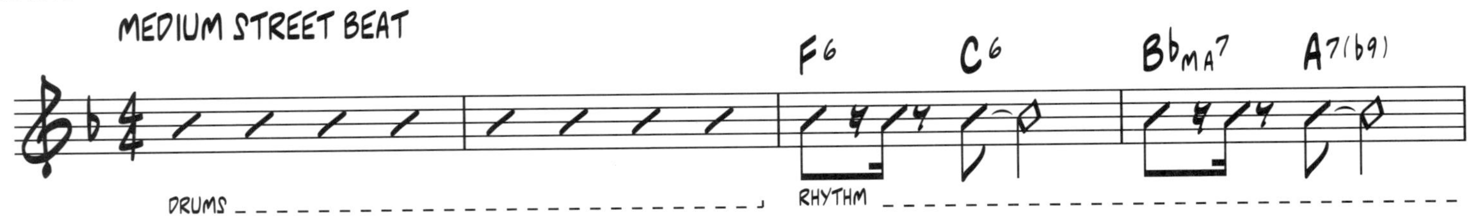

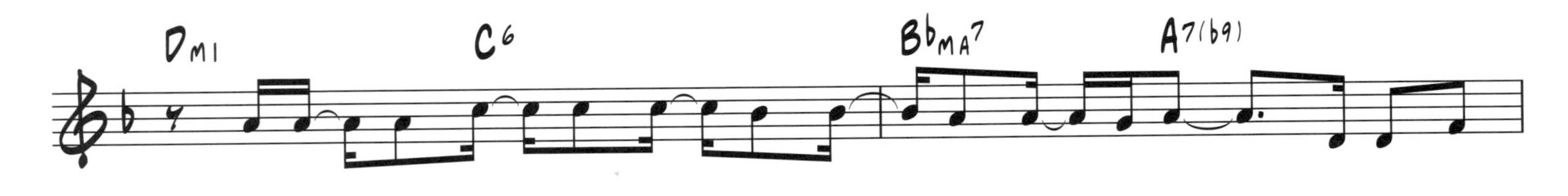

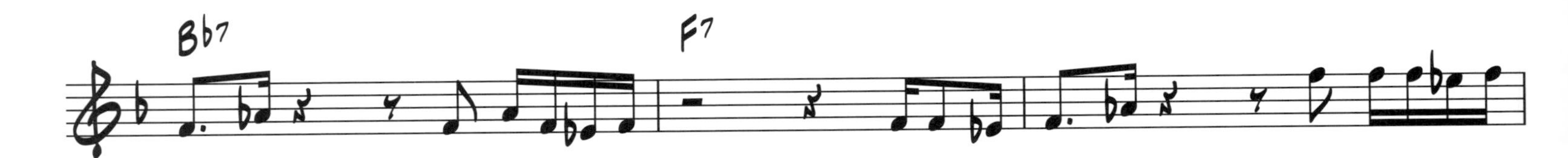

SOLO
6X'S
LAST X ONLY
DRUM FILL

CD

11: SPLIT TRACK/MELODY
12: FULL STEREO TRACK

HOMEWARD BOUND

WORDS AND MUSIC BY
PAUL SIMON

CMA7
FMA7
CMA7
FMA7
SOLO
CMA7
EMI7/B
GMI6/Bb
A7
A7(b9)
DMI7
DMI7/C
BMI7(b5)
Bb7
AMI7
AMI7/G
FMA7
FMA7/G
C6
G7SUS
GbMI7(b5)
FMA7
FMA7/G
C6
G7SUS
GbMI7(b5)
FMA7
FMA7/G
CMA7
/B
AMI7
/G
FMA7
/E
DMI7
G7SUS
CMA7
FMA7
CMA7
FMA7
D.S. AL CODA
CODA
DMI7/G
CMA7
FMA7
C/Bb
EbMA7
AbMA7
Db6(b5)
CMA7

CD

13 : SPLIT TRACK/MELODY
14 : FULL STEREO TRACK

LOVES ME LIKE A ROCK

WORDS AND MUSIC BY
PAUL SIMON

C VERSION

SOLOS (2 CHORUSES)
Gb7
Cb7
Gb7
Cb7
Gb7
Cb7
Bb7
Ab7
G7
LAST X ONLY
G7 C7 G7
G7 C7 G7
C7
C7SUS D7SUS
G7 F7 G7
G7 C7 G7
G7 C7 G7
C7
C7SUS D7SUS
EMI7 A7 D7SUS
G7
EMI7
C7
G7
C7
F7SUS C7
G7
F#+7(b9)
F7
E+7(#9)
EbMA7
N.C.
G7
DRUMS

CD

15 : SPLIT TRACK/MELODY
16 : FULL STEREO TRACK

MRS. ROBINSON

WORDS AND MUSIC BY
PAUL SIMON

C VERSION

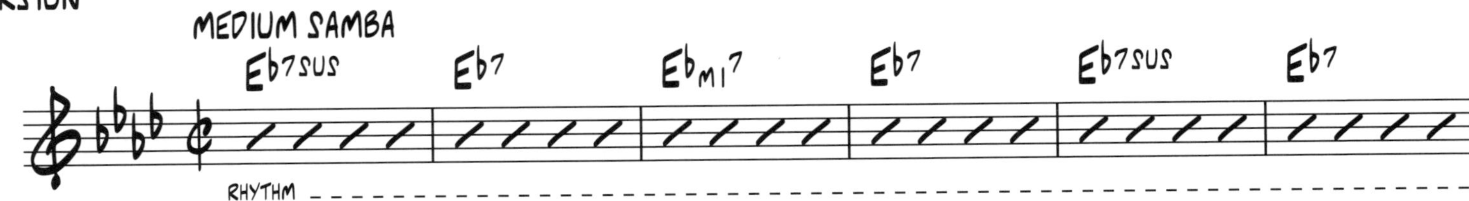

F7
Eb7
AbMA7
FMI7
AbMA7
FMI7
Db6
BbMI7
Eb7
AbMA7
FMI7
AbMA7
FMI7
Db6
BbMI7
SOLOS (12 CHORUSES)
F7SUS
F7
FMI7
F7
Eb7SUS
Eb7
1ST X ONLY
EbMI7
Eb7
F7
N.C.
Eb7
N.C.
EMA7
AMA7(b5)
AbMI7
DRUM FILL
DRUM FILL

CD

17 : SPLIT TRACK/MELODY

18 : FULL STEREO TRACK

SLIP SLIDIN' AWAY

WORDS AND MUSIC BY
PAUL SIMON

C VERSION

TO CODA
F6 C6 Bb6 C6 F6
SOLOS (2 CHORUSES)
F6 Dmi7
Bbma7 Gmi7 C7sus C#o
Dmi7 Eb7
D.S. AL CODA
F6/C C7sus F/A Bb7sus C7sus
3
LAST X ONLY
CODA
F6 Dmi7 Bbma7 Gmi7
C7sus C#o Dmi7 Dbma7(b5)
Bbma7 Ami7 Gmi7 C7sus N.C. Ebma7(b5)

CD
19 : SPLIT TRACK/MELODY
20 : FULL STEREO TRACK
STILL CRAZY AFTER ALL THESE YEARS
C VERSION
WORDS AND MUSIC BY
PAUL SIMON
SLOW GOSPEL WALTZ
CMA7 GMA7 G6 GMI/D CMI7
PIANO
EbMA7 F7 Bb Eb/Bb Bb
PLAY
mf
Bb6 Bb7/D Eb7 Ab7
Bb7 AMI7(b5) D7SUS D7 GMI7 Gb7
FMI7 Bb7 Eb7 E07
Bb/F F7 F#07 GMI7 E07

Bb/F F7
1. Bb Eb/Bb Bb
2. Bb7SUS Bb7 Bb7SUS Bb7/Ab G+7(b9)

CMA7
GMA7 G6
GMI/D
BMI7
E7SUS
AMA7
Ab7SUS
GMI7
DMA7 EbMA7
DMA7 EbMA7
Bb7(b5) Bb7
EbMA7
D7
EbMA7
D7
EbMA7
D7 C7
SOLOS (6 CHORUSES)
Bb6
Bb7/D
Eb7
Bb7
Eb/Bb
Bb7
Bb6
Bb7/D
Eb7
Ab7
Bb7
3
AMI7(b5)
D7SUS
D7
G7SUS
C7
C7/E
F7
F#o7
C/G
G7
G#o7
AMI7
/G
F#o7
C/G
C7
F
Bb/F
F
F#o7
C/G
G7
AbMA7
Bb6
C(ADD2)
RIT.

CD

BRIDGE OVER TROUBLED WATER

WORDS AND MUSIC BY
PAUL SIMON

GMI7/C FMA7 /E
F7/Eb CMI6 B+7 BbMA7 B+7 CMI7 F7 /A
BbMA7 C/Bb AMI7 DMI7 /C BbMA7 A+7(b9)
DMI7 CMI6 B+7 BbMA7 C/Bb AMI7 DMI7
GMI7 GMI7/C FMA7 Eb6
LAST X ONLY
FMA7 Eb6 E6 FMA7
Eb6 FMA7 BbMA7
FMA7 EMI7 DMI7 GMI7/C
FMA7 /E F7/Eb CMI6 B+7
BbMA7 B+7 CMI7 F7 /A BbMA7 C/Bb
AMI7 DMI7 /C BbMA7 A7(b9) DMI7 CMI6 F7
Bb6 BbMA7 C/Bb A+7(b9) DMI7 GMI7 GMI7/C
Eb6 GMI7/C G/F

Bb VERSION

CECILIA

WORDS AND MUSIC BY
PAUL SIMON

N.C./G
G7ADD4
G7
PIANO
F/G
G7
D.S. AL CODA
CODA
G7ADD4
G7
F7/G
G7
G7ADD4
G7
F7/G
G7

CD

5 : SPLIT TRACK/MELODY
6 : FULL STEREO TRACK

Bb VERSION

EL CONDOR PASA

(IF I COULD)

ENGLISH LYRIC BY PAUL SIMON
MUSICAL ARRANGEMENT BY JORGE MILCHBERG
AND DANIEL ROBLES

SOLO
DMI7 G7 DMI7 G7 DMI7 G7 DMI7 G7
DMI7 G7 DMI7 G7 DMI7 G7 DMI7 DMI7/C
BbMA7 FMA7 B7
BbMA7 AMI7 GMI7 FMA7 A+7(#9)
DMI7 G7 DMI7 G7 DMI7 G7 DMI7 G7
DMI7 G7 DMI7 G7 DMI7 G7 /F Eb7(b5)
D.S. AL CODA
CODA
Eb7(b5) DMI6

CD

7: SPLIT TRACK/MELODY

8: FULL STEREO TRACK

Bb VERSION

THE 59TH STREET BRIDGE SONG

(FEELIN' GROOVY)

WORDS AND MUSIC BY
PAUL SIMON

MEDIUM LIGHT ROCK

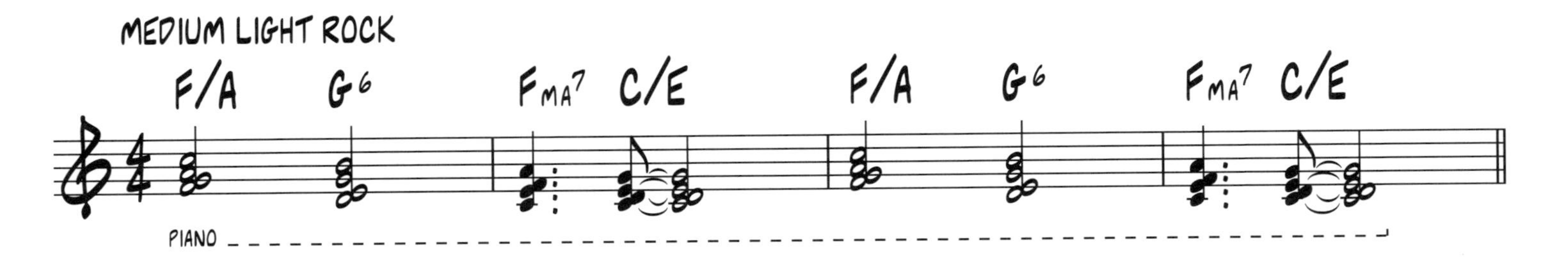

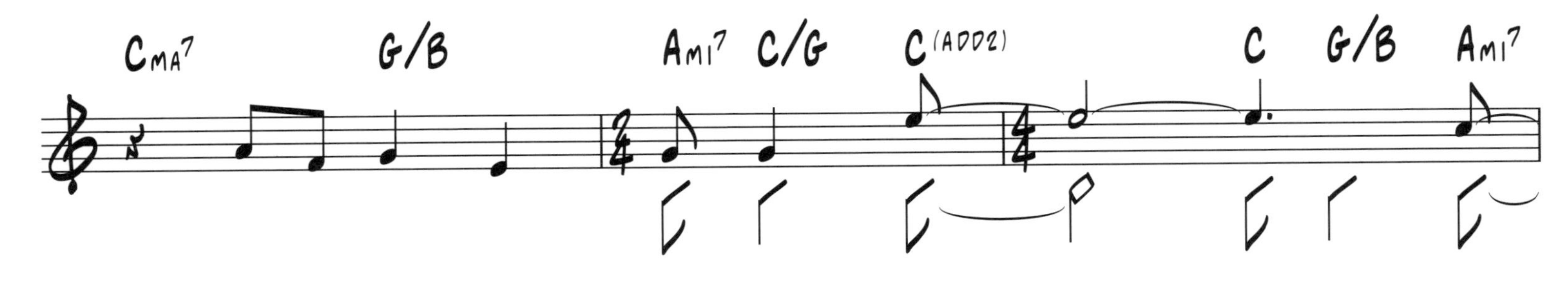

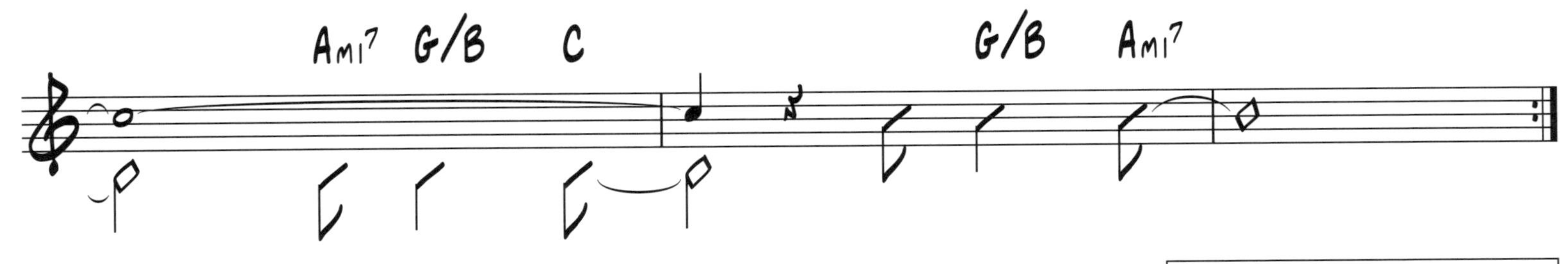

4.
Ami7/D D/C G/B A6 Gma7 D/F# C/E Dma7
C(ADD2) Bmi7 Ami7 G(ADD2) F(ADD2) Emi7 Dma7 A/C#
Bmi7 D/A D(ADD2) D A/C# Bmi7 A/C# D(ADD2)
D A/C# Bmi7 G/B A6 Gma7 D/F#
C/E Dma7 C(ADD2) Bmi7 Ami7 G(ADD2) F(ADD2) Emi7
Dma7 A/C# Bmi7 D/A D(ADD2) D A/C# Bmi7
A/C# D(ADD2) D A/C# Bmi7

CD

9: SPLIT TRACK/MELODY

10: FULL STEREO TRACK

FIFTY WAYS TO LEAVE YOUR LOVER

Bb VERSION

WORDS AND MUSIC BY
PAUL SIMON

SOLO
G6 D6 CMA7 B7(b9) EMI B7/D# G+ B7(b9)
EMI D6 CMA7 B7(b9) EMI AMI EMI
EMI AMI EMI G7 Bb7 C7
G7 Bb7 C7 G7
6X'S F7 G7
LAST X ONLY
G7 Bb7 C7
G7 Bb7
C7 C#7(b5) C7 B+7(#9) Bb7
A7(#9) Ab7(b5) E7(b5) F7 F#7 G7 Ab7 G7
DRUM FILL

CD

11: SPLIT TRACK/MELODY
12: FULL STEREO TRACK

HOMEWARD BOUND

WORDS AND MUSIC BY
PAUL SIMON

B♭ VERSION

DMA7
GMA7
DMA7
GMA7
SOLO
DMA7
F#MI7/C#
AMI6/C
B7
B7(b9)
EMI7
EMI7/D
C#MI7(b5)
C7
BMI7
BMI7/A
GMA7
GMA7/A
D6
A7SUS
AbMI7(b5)
GMA7
GMA7/A
D6
A7SUS
AbMI7(b5)
GMA7
GMA7/A
DMA7
/C#
BMI7
/A
GMA7
/F#
EMI7
A7SUS
DMA7
GMA7
DMA7
GMA7
D.S. AL CODA
CODA
EMI7/A
DMA7
GMA7
D/C
FMA7
BbMA7
E♭6(b5)
DMA7

CD

13: SPLIT TRACK/MELODY

14: FULL STEREO TRACK

LOVES ME LIKE A ROCK

WORDS AND MUSIC BY
PAUL SIMON

B♭ VERSION

SOLOS (2 CHORUSES)
Ab7
Db7
Ab7
Db7
Ab7
Db7
C7
Bb7
A7
LAST X ONLY
A7
D7
A7
A7
D7
A7
D7
D7SUS
E7SUS
A7
G7
A7
A7
D7
A7
A7
D7
A7
D7
D7SUS
E7SUS
F#MI7
B7
E7SUS
A7
F#MI7
D7
A7
D7
G7SUS
D7
A7
G#+7(b9)
G7
F#+7(#9)
FMA7
N.C.
A7
DRUMS

CD
15 : SPLIT TRACK/MELODY
16 : FULL STEREO TRACK

MRS. ROBINSON

WORDS AND MUSIC BY
PAUL SIMON

MEDIUM SAMBA

G7
F7
B♭MA7
GMI7
B♭MA7
GMI7
E♭6
CMI7
F7
B♭MA7
GMI7
B♭MA7
GMI7
E♭6
CMI7
SOLOS (12 CHORUSES)
G7SUS
G7
GMI7
G7
F7SUS
F7
1ST X ONLY
FMI7
F7
G7
N.C.
F7
N.C.
F♯MA7
BMA7(♭5)
B♭MI7
DRUM FILL
DRUM FILL

CD

17 : SPLIT TRACK/MELODY

18 : FULL STEREO TRACK

SLIP SLIDIN' AWAY

WORDS AND MUSIC BY
PAUL SIMON

B♭ VERSION

TO CODA
G6
D6
C6
D6
G6
SOLOS (2 CHORUSES)
G6
EMI7
CMA7
AMI7
D7SUS
D#o
EMI7
F7
D.S. AL CODA
G6/D
D7SUS
G/B
C7SUS
D7SUS
3
LAST X ONLY
CODA
G6
EMI7
CMA7
AMI7
D7SUS
D#o
EMI7
EbMA7(b5)
CMA7
BMI7
AMI7
D7SUS
N.C.
FMA7(b5)

STILL CRAZY AFTER ALL THESE YEARS

WORDS AND MUSIC BY
PAUL SIMON

B♭ VERSION

DMA7
AMA7 A6
AMI/E
C#MI7
F#7SUS
BMA7
Bb7SUS
AMI7
EMA7 FMA7
EMA7 FMA7
C7(b5) C7
FMA7
E7
FMA7
E7
FMA7
E7 D7
SOLOS (6 CHORUSES)
C6
C7/E
F7
C7
F/C
C7
C6
C7/E
F7
Bb7
C7
BMI7(b5)
E7SUS E7
A7SUS
D7
D7/F#
G7
G#o7
D/A
A7
A#o7
BMI7 /A
G#o7
D/A
D7
G
C/G G
G#o7
D/A
A7
BbMA7
C6
D(ADD2)
RIT.

BRIDGE OVER TROUBLED WATER

WORDS AND MUSIC BY
PAUL SIMON

DMI7/G CMA7 /B
C7/Bb GMI6 F#+7 FMA7 F#+7 GMI7 C7 /E
FMA7 G/F EMI7 AMI7 /G FMA7 E+7(b9)
AMI7 GMI6 F#+7 FMA7 G/F EMI7 AMI7
DMI7 DMI7/G CMA7 Bb6
LAST X ONLY
CMA7 Bb6 B6 CMA7
Bb6 CMA7 FMA7
CMA7 BMI7 AMI7 DMI7/G
CMA7 /B C7/Bb GMI6 F#+7
FMA7 F#+7 GMI7 C7 /E FMA7 G/F
EMI7 AMI7 /G FMA7 E7(b9) AMI7 GMI6 C7
F6 FMA7 G/F E+7(b9) AMI7 DMI7 DMI7/G
3
Bb6 DMI7/G D/C

CD

3: SPLIT TRACK/MELODY

4: FULL STEREO TRACK

E♭ VERSION

CECILIA

WORDS AND MUSIC BY
PAUL SIMON

N.C./D
D7ADD4
D7
PIANO
C/D
D7
D.S. AL CODA
CODA
D7ADD4
D7
C7/D
D7
D7ADD4
D7
C7/D
D7

CD

5 : SPLIT TRACK/MELODY

6 : FULL STEREO TRACK

Eb VERSION

EL CONDOR PASA

(IF I COULD)

ENGLISH LYRIC BY PAUL SIMON
MUSICAL ARRANGEMENT BY JORGE MILCHBERG
AND DANIEL ROBLES

SOLO
Ami7 D7 Ami7 D7 Ami7 D7 Ami7 D7
Ami7 D7 Ami7 D7 Ami7 D7 Ami7 Ami7/G
Fma7 Cma7 F#7
Fma7 Emi7 Dmi7 Cma7 E+7(#9)
Ami7 D7 Ami7 D7 Ami7 D7 Ami7 D7
Ami7 D7 Ami7 D7 Ami7 D7 /C Bb7(b5) D.S. AL CODA
CODA
Bb7(b5) Ami6

CD

: SPLIT TRACK/MELODY

: FULL STEREO TRACK

Eb VERSION

THE 59TH STREET BRIDGE SONG

(FEELIN' GROOVY)

WORDS AND MUSIC BY
PAUL SIMON

4.
Emi7/A A/G D/F# E6 Dma7 A/C# G/B Ama7
G(ADD2) F#mi7 Emi7 D(ADD2) C(ADD2) Bmi7 Ama7 E/G#
F#mi7 A/E A(ADD2) A E/G# F#mi7 E/G# A(ADD2)
A E/G# F#mi7 D/F# E6 Dma7 A/C#
G/B Ama7 G(ADD2) F#mi7 Emi7 D(ADD2) C(ADD2) Bmi7
Ama7 E/G# F#mi7 A/E A(ADD2) A E/G# F#mi7
E/G# A(ADD2) A E/G# F#mi7

FIFTY WAYS TO LEAVE YOUR LOVER

WORDS AND MUSIC BY
PAUL SIMON

Eb VERSION

SOLO
D6 A6
GMA7 F#7(b9)
BMI F#7/A#
D+ F#7(b9)
BMI A6
GMA7 F#7(b9)
BMI EMI
BMI
BMI EMI
BMI
D7
F7
G7
D7
F7
G7
D7
6X'S
C7
D7
LAST X ONLY
D7
F7
G7
D7
F7
G7
G#7(b5) G7
F#+7(#9) F7
E7(#9) Eb7(b5)
B7(b5) C7 C#7
D7
Eb7
D7
DRUM FILL

CD

11: SPLIT TRACK/MELODY

12: FULL STEREO TRACK

HOMEWARD BOUND

WORDS AND MUSIC BY
PAUL SIMON

E♭ VERSION

AMA7
DMA7
AMA7
DMA7
SOLO
AMA7
C#MI7/G#
EMI6/G
F#7
F#7(b9)
BMI7
BMI7/A
G#MI7(b5)
G7
F#MI7
F#MI7/E
DMA7
DMA7/E
A6
E7SUS
EbMI7(b5)
DMA7
DMA7/E
A6
E7SUS
EbMI7(b5)
DMA7
DMA7/E
AMA7
/G#
F#MI7
/E
DMA7
/C#
BMI7
E7SUS
AMA7
DMA7
AMA7
DMA7
D.S. AL CODA
CODA
BMI7/E
AMA7
DMA7
A/G
CMA7
FMA7
Bb6(b5)
AMA7

CD

13: SPLIT TRACK/MELODY

14: FULL STEREO TRACK

LOVES ME LIKE A ROCK

WORDS AND MUSIC BY
PAUL SIMON

E♭ VERSION

SOLOS (2 CHORUSES)
Eb7 Ab7 Eb7 Ab7 Eb7
Ab7 G7 F7 E7
LAST X ONLY
E7 A7 E7 E7 A7 E7
A7 A7SUS B7SUS E7 D7 E7
E7 A7 E7 E7 A7 E7
A7 A7SUS B7SUS C#MI7 F#7 B7SUS
E7 C#MI7 A7 E7
A7 D7SUS A7 E7 D#+7(b9)
D7 C#+7(#9) CMA7 N.C.
E7
DRUMS

MRS. ROBINSON

CD
15: SPLIT TRACK/MELODY
16: FULL STEREO TRACK

WORDS AND MUSIC BY
PAUL SIMON

D7
C7
FMA7
DMI7
FMA7
DMI7
Bb6
GMI7
C7
FMA7
DMI7
FMA7
DMI7
Bb6
GMI7
SOLOS (12 CHORUSES)
D7SUS
D7
DMI7
D7
C7SUS
C7
1ST X ONLY
CMI7
C7
D7
N.C.
C7
N.C.
C#MA7
F#MA7(b5)
FMI7
DRUM FILL
DRUM FILL

CD

- 17 : SPLIT TRACK/MELODY
- 18 : FULL STEREO TRACK

SLIP SLIDIN' AWAY

WORDS AND MUSIC BY
PAUL SIMON

Eb VERSION

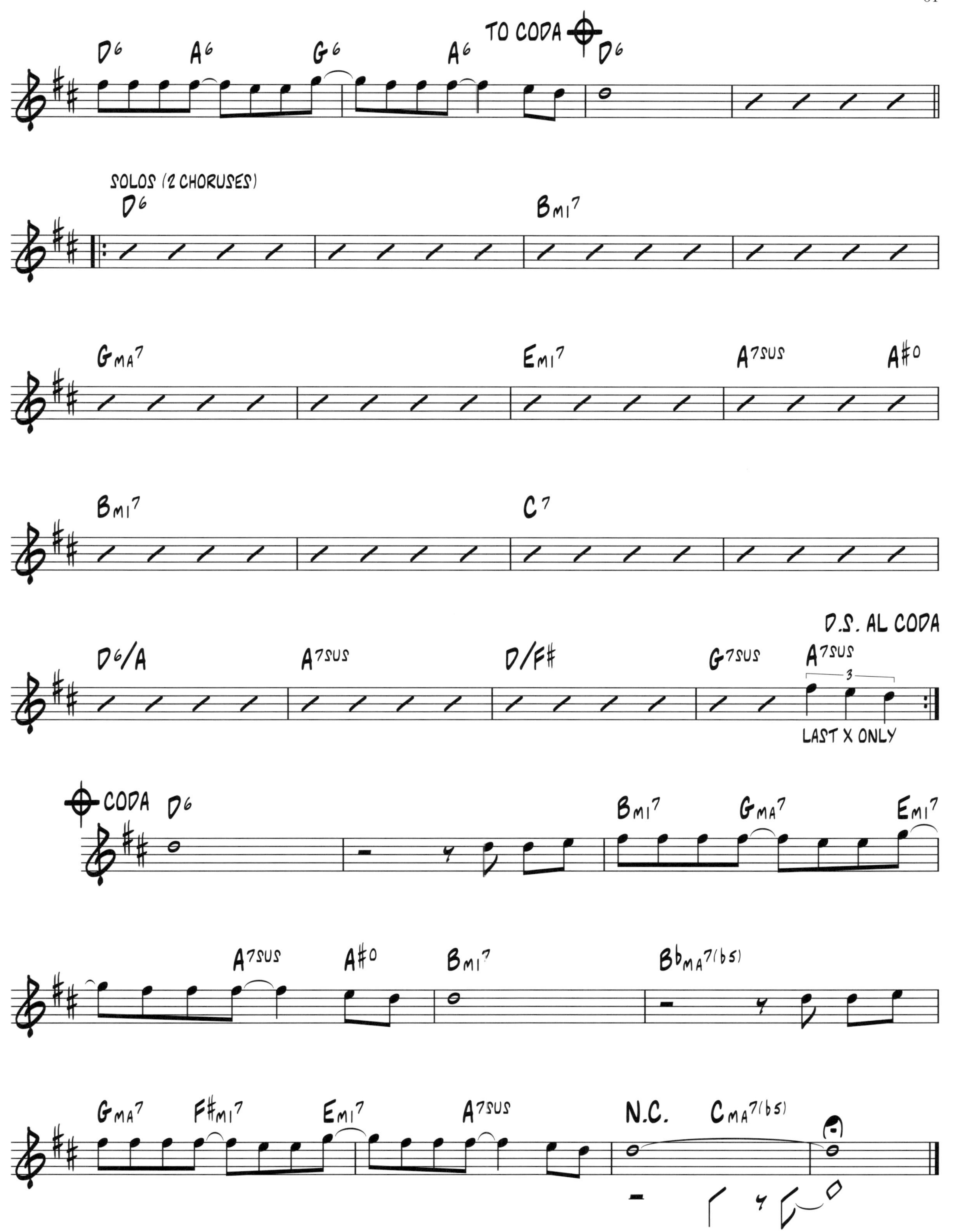

TO CODA
D6 A6 G6 A6 D6
SOLOS (2 CHORUSES)
D6 BMI7
GMA7 EMI7 A7SUS A#o
BMI7 C7
D.S. AL CODA
D6/A A7SUS D/F# G7SUS A7SUS
3
LAST X ONLY
CODA D6 BMI7 GMA7 EMI7
A7SUS A#o BMI7 BbMA7(b5)
GMA7 F#MI7 EMI7 A7SUS N.C. CMA7(b5)

CD
19 : SPLIT TRACK/MELODY
20 : FULL STEREO TRACK
STILL CRAZY AFTER ALL THESE YEARS
Eb VERSION
WORDS AND MUSIC BY
PAUL SIMON
SLOW GOSPEL WALTZ
AMA7
EMA7
E6
EMI/B
AMI7
PIANO
CMA7
D7
G
C/G
G
PLAY
mf
G6
G7/B
C7
F7
G7
F#MI7(b5)
B7SUS
B7
EMI7
Eb7
DMI7
4
G7
C7
C#o7
3
G/D
D7
D#o7
EMI7
C#o7
G/D
D7
1.
G
C/G
G

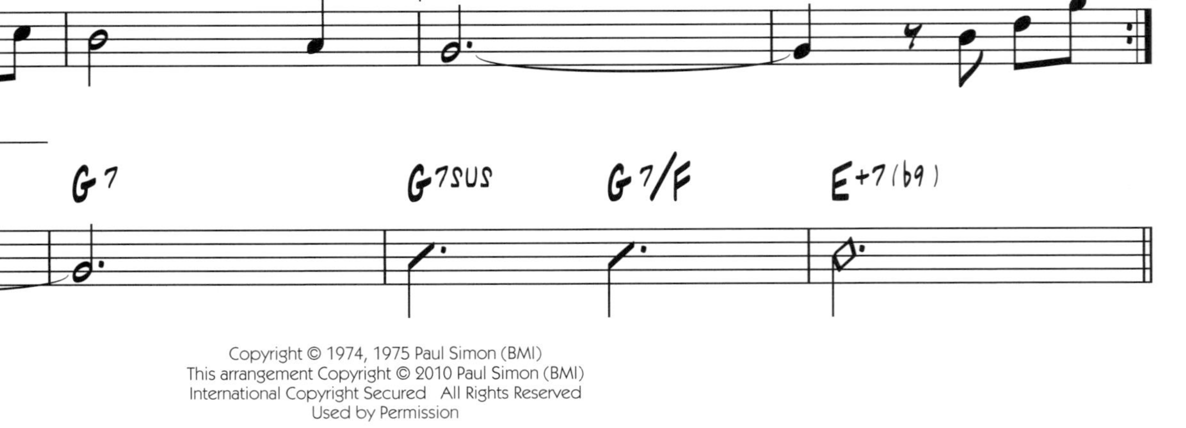
2.
G7SUS
G7
G7SUS
G7/F
E+7(b9)

AMA7 EMA7 E6 EMI/B G#MI7
C#7SUS F#MA7 F7SUS EMI7 BMA7 CMA7
BMA7 CMA7 G7(b5) G7 CMA7 B7
CMA7 B7 CMA7 B7 A7
SOLOS (6 CHORUSES)
G6 G7/B
C7 G7 C/G G7
G6 G7/B C7 F7 G7
3
F#MI7(b5) B7SUS B7 E7SUS A7 A7/C#
D7 D#O7 A/E E7 E#O7 F#MI7 /E
D#O7 A/E A7 D G/D D D#O7
A/E E7 FMA7 G6 A(ADD2)
RIT.

CD
: SPLIT TRACK/MELODY
2 : FULL STEREO TRACK

BRIDGE OVER TROUBLED WATER

WORDS AND MUSIC BY
PAUL SIMON

C VERSION

MEDIUM SAMBA

Ebma7 Db6 Ebma7

RHYTHM LAST X ONLY mf

Db6 Ebma7 Db6

Ebma7 Abma7 Ebma7

Dmi7 Cmi7 Fmi7/Bb 3

Ebma7 /D Eb7/Db Bbmi6 A+7 Abma7 A+7

Bbmi7 Eb7 /G Abma7 Bb/Ab Gmi7 Cmi7 /Bb

Abma7 G+7(b9) Cmi7 Bbmi6 A+7 Abma7 Bb/Ab Gmi7

Cmi7 Fmi7 Fmi7/Bb Db6

SOLO

Ebma7 Db6 Ebma7

Db6 Ebma7

Abma7 Ebma7 Dmi7 Cmi7

FMI7/Bb EbMA7 /D
Eb7/Db BbMI6 A+7 AbMA7 A+7 BbMI7 Eb7 /G
AbMA7 Bb/Ab GMI7 CMI7 /Bb AbMA7 G+7(b9)
CMI7 BbMI6 A+7 AbMA7 Bb/Ab GMI7 CMI7
FMI7 FMI7/Bb EbMA7 Db6
LAST X ONLY
EbMA7 Db6 D6 EbMA7
Db6 EbMA7 AbMA7
EbMA7 DMI7 CMI7 FMI7/Bb
EbMA7 /D Eb7/Db BbMI6 A+7
AbMA7 A+7 BbMI7 Eb7 /G AbMA7 Bb/Ab
GMI7 CMI7 /Bb AbMA7 G7(b9) CMI7 BbMI6 Eb7
Ab6 AbMA7 Bb/Ab G+7(b9) CMI7 FMI7 FMI7/Bb
3
Db6 FMI7/Bb F/Eb

CECILIA

WORDS AND MUSIC BY
PAUL SIMON

N.C./F
F7ADD4
F7
PIANO
Eb/F
F7
D.S. AL CODA
CODA
F7ADD4
F7
Eb7/F
F7
F7ADD4
F7
Eb7/F
F7

CD

5 : SPLIT TRACK/MELODY

6 : FULL STEREO TRACK

EL CONDOR PASA

(IF I COULD)

C VERSION

ENGLISH LYRIC BY PAUL SIMON
MUSICAL ARRANGEMENT BY JORGE MILCHBERG
AND DANIEL ROBLES

SOLO
CMI7 F7 CMI7 F7 CMI7 F7 CMI7 F7
CMI7 F7 CMI7 F7 CMI7 F7 CMI7 CMI7/Bb
AbMA7 EbMA7 A7
AbMA7 GMI7 FMI7 EbMA7 G+7(#9)
CMI7 F7 CMI7 F7 CMI7 F7 CMI7 F7
CMI7 F7 CMI7 F7 CMI7 F7 /Eb Db7(b5) D.S. AL CODA
CODA
Db7(b5) CMI6

CD

C VERSION

THE 59TH STREET BRIDGE SONG

(FEELIN' GROOVY)

WORDS AND MUSIC BY
PAUL SIMON

4.
Gmi7/C C/Bb F/A G6 Fma7 C/E Bb/D Cma7
Bb(add2) Ami7 Gmi7 F(add2) Eb(add2) Dmi7 Cma7 G/B
Ami7 C/G C(add2) C G/B Ami7 G/B C(add2)
C G/B Ami7 F/A G6 Fma7 C/E
Bb/D Cma7 Bb(add2) Ami7 Gmi7 F(add2) Eb(add2) Dmi7
Cma7 G/B Ami7 C/G C(add2) C G/B Ami7
G/B C(add2) C G/B Ami7

FIFTY WAYS TO LEAVE YOUR LOVER

CD
9: SPLIT TRACK/MELODY
10: FULL STEREO TRACK

WORDS AND MUSIC BY
PAUL SIMON

C VERSION

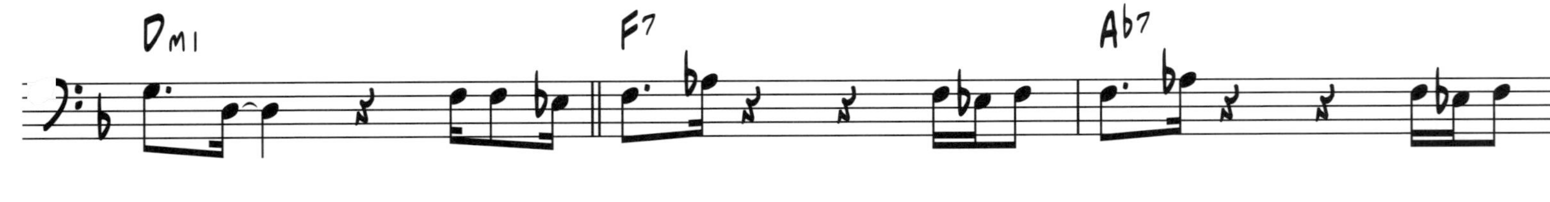

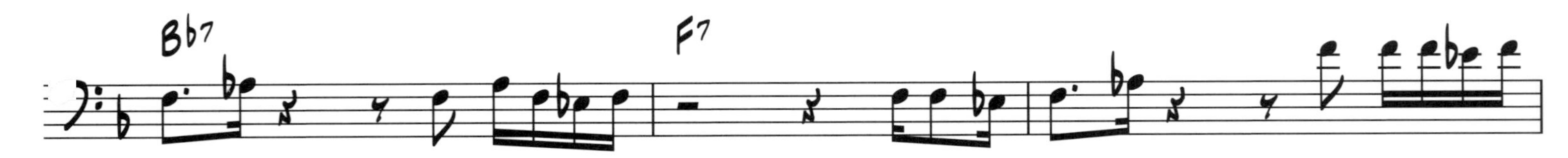

SOLO
F6 C6
Bbma7 A7(b9)
Dmi A7/C#
F+ A7(b9)
Dmi C6
Bbma7 A7(b9)
Dmi Gmi
Dmi
Dmi Gmi
Dmi
F7
Ab7
Bb7
F7
Ab7
Bb7
F7
6X'S Eb7
F7
LAST X ONLY
F7
Ab7
Bb7
F7
Ab7
Bb7
B7(b5) Bb7
A+7(#9) Ab7
G7(#9) Gb7(b5)
D7(b5) Eb7 E7
F7
Gb7
F7
3
DRUM FILL

CD

: SPLIT TRACK/MELODY

12: FULL STEREO TRACK

HOMEWARD BOUND

WORDS AND MUSIC BY
PAUL SIMON

CMA7
FMA7
CMA7
FMA7
SOLO
CMA7
EMI7/B
GMI6/Bb
A7
A7(b9)
DMI7
DMI7/C
BMI7(b5)
Bb7
AMI7
AMI7/G
FMA7
FMA7/G
C6
G7SUS
GbMI7(b5)
FMA7
FMA7/G
C6
G7SUS
GbMI7(b5)
FMA7
FMA7/G
CMA7
/B
AMI7
/G
FMA7
/E
DMI7
G7SUS
CMA7
FMA7
CMA7
FMA7
D.S. AL CODA
CODA
DMI7/G
CMA7
FMA7
C/Bb
EbMA7
AbMA7
Db6(b5)
CMA7

CD

13: SPLIT TRACK/MELODY

14: FULL STEREO TRACK

LOVES ME LIKE A ROCK

WORDS AND MUSIC BY
PAUL SIMON

C VERSION

SOLOS (2 CHORUSES)
Gb7
Cb7
Gb7
Cb7
Gb7
Cb7
Bb7
Ab7
G7
LAST X ONLY
G7
C7
G7
C7sus
D7sus
F7
Emi7
A7
D7sus
F7sus
F#+7(b9)
E+7(#9)
Ebma7
N.C.
DRUMS

CD

MRS. ROBINSON

WORDS AND MUSIC BY
PAUL SIMON

C VERSION

F7
Eb7
AbMA7
FMI7
AbMA7
FMI7
Db6
BbMI7
Eb7
AbMA7
FMI7
AbMA7
FMI7
Db6
BbMI7
SOLOS (12 CHORUSES)
F7SUS
F7
FMI7
F7
Eb7SUS
Eb7
1ST X ONLY
EbMI7
Eb7
F7
N.C.
Eb7
N.C.
EMA7
AMA7(b5)
AbMI7
DRUM FILL
DRUM FILL

CD

17 : SPLIT TRACK/MELODY

18 : FULL STEREO TRACK

SLIP SLIDIN' AWAY

WORDS AND MUSIC BY
PAUL SIMON

F6 C6 Bb6 C6 TO CODA F6
SOLOS (2 CHORUSES)
F6 Dmi7
BbMA7 Gmi7 C7SUS C#o
Dmi7 Eb7
D.S. AL CODA
F6/C C7SUS F/A Bb7SUS C7SUS
3
LAST X ONLY
CODA F6 Dmi7 BbMA7 Gmi7
C7SUS C#o Dmi7 DbMA7(b5)
BbMA7 Ami7 Gmi7 C7SUS N.C. EbMA7(b5)

STILL CRAZY AFTER ALL THESE YEARS

CMA7 GMA7 G6 GMI/D BMI7
E7SUS AMA7 Ab7SUS GMI7 DMA7 EbMA7
DMA7 EbMA7 Bb7(b5) Bb7 EbMA7 D7
SOLOS (6 CHORUSES)
EbMA7 D7 EbMA7 D7 C7 Bb6 Bb7/D
Eb7 Bb7 Eb/Bb Bb7
Bb6 Bb7/D Eb7 Ab7 Bb7
AMI7(b5) D7SUS D7 G7SUS C7 C7/E
F7 F#o7 C/G G7 G#o7 AMI7 /G
F#o7 C/G C7 F Bb/F F F#o7
C/G G7 AbMA7 Bb6 C(ADD2)
RIT.

Presenting the Hal Leonard JAZZ PLAY-ALONG® SERIES

For use with all B-flat, E-flat, Bass Clef and C instruments, the Jazz Play-Along® Series is the ultimate learning tool for all jazz musicians. With musician-friendly lead sheets, melody cues, and other split-track choices on the included CD, these first-of-a-kind packages help you master improvisation while playing some of the greatest tunes of all time. FOR STUDY, each tune includes a split track with: melody cue with proper style and inflection • professional rhythm tracks • choruses for soloing • removable bass part • removable piano part. FOR PERFORMANCE, each tune also has: an additional full stereo accompaniment track (no melody) • additional choruses for soloing.

1. **DUKE ELLINGTON**
   00841644 .... $16.95
2. **MILES DAVIS**
   00841645 .... $16.95
3. **THE BLUES**
   00841646 .... $16.99
4. **JAZZ BALLADS**
   00841691 .... $16.99
5. **BEST OF BEBOP**
   00841689 .... $16.99
6. **JAZZ CLASSICS WITH EASY CHANGES**
   00841690 .... $16.99
7. **ESSENTIAL JAZZ STANDARDS**
   00843000 .... $16.99
8. **ANTONIO CARLOS JOBIM AND THE ART OF THE BOSSA NOVA**
   00843001 .... $16.95
9. **DIZZY GILLESPIE**
   00843002 .... $16.99
10. **DISNEY CLASSICS**
    00843003 .... $16.99
11. **RODGERS AND HART FAVORITES**
    00843004 .... $16.99
12. **ESSENTIAL JAZZ CLASSICS**
    00843005 .... $16.99
13. **JOHN COLTRANE**
    00843006 .... $16.95
14. **IRVING BERLIN**
    00843007 .... $15.99
15. **RODGERS & HAMMERSTEIN**
    00843008 .... $15.99
16. **COLE PORTER**
    00843009 .... $15.95
17. **COUNT BASIE**
    00843010 .... $16.95
18. **HAROLD ARLEN**
    00843011 .... $15.95
19. **COOL JAZZ**
    00843012 .... $15.95
20. **CHRISTMAS CAROLS**
    00843080 .... $14.95
21. **RODGERS AND HART CLASSICS**
    00843014 .... $14.95
22. **WAYNE SHORTER**
    00843015 .... $16.95
23. **LATIN JAZZ**
    00843016 .... $16.95
24. **EARLY JAZZ STANDARDS**
    00843017 .... $14.95
25. **CHRISTMAS JAZZ**
    00843018 .... $16.95
26. **CHARLIE PARKER**
    00843019 .... $16.95
27. **GREAT JAZZ STANDARDS**
    00843020 .... $15.99
28. **BIG BAND ERA**
    00843021 .... $15.99
29. **LENNON AND MCCARTNEY**
    00843022 .... $16.95
30. **BLUES' BEST**
    00843023 .... $15.99
31. **JAZZ IN THREE**
    00843024 .... $15.99
32. **BEST OF SWING**
    00843025 .... $15.99
33. **SONNY ROLLINS**
    00843029 .... $15.95
34. **ALL TIME STANDARDS**
    00843030 .... $15.99
35. **BLUESY JAZZ**
    00843031 .... $15.99
36. **HORACE SILVER**
    00843032 .... $16.99
37. **BILL EVANS**
    00843033 .... $16.95
38. **YULETIDE JAZZ**
    00843034 .... $16.95
39. **"ALL THE THINGS YOU ARE" & MORE JEROME KERN SONGS**
    00843035 .... $15.99
40. **BOSSA NOVA**
    00843036 .... $15.99
41. **CLASSIC DUKE ELLINGTON**
    00843037 .... $16.99
42. **GERRY MULLIGAN FAVORITES**
    00843038 .... $16.99
43. **GERRY MULLIGAN CLASSICS**
    00843039 .... $16.95
44. **OLIVER NELSON**
    00843040 .... $16.95
45. **JAZZ AT THE MOVIES**
    00843041 .... $15.99
46. **BROADWAY JAZZ STANDARDS**
    00843042 .... $15.99
47. **CLASSIC JAZZ BALLADS**
    00843043 .... $15.99
48. **BEBOP CLASSICS**
    00843044 .... $16.99
49. **MILES DAVIS STANDARDS**
    00843045 .... $16.95
50. **GREAT JAZZ CLASSICS**
    00843046 .... $15.99
51. **UP-TEMPO JAZZ**
    00843047 .... $15.99
52. **STEVIE WONDER**
    00843048 .... $15.95
53. **RHYTHM CHANGES**
    00843049 .... $15.99

54. **"MOONLIGHT IN VERMONT" AND OTHER GREAT STANDARDS**
00843050 .... $15.99

55. **BENNY GOLSON**
00843052 .... $15.95

56. **"GEORGIA ON MY MIND" & OTHER SONGS BY HOAGY CARMICHAEL**
00843056 .... $15.99

57. **VINCE GUARALDI**
00843057 .... $16.99

58. **MORE LENNON AND MCCARTNEY**
00843059 .... $15.99

59. **SOUL JAZZ**
00843060 .... $15.99

60. **DEXTER GORDON**
00843061 .... $15.95

61. **MONGO SANTAMARIA**
00843062 .... $15.95

62. **JAZZ-ROCK FUSION**
00843063 .... $14.95

63. **CLASSICAL JAZZ**
00843064 .... $14.95

64. **TV TUNES**
00843065 .... $14.95

65. **SMOOTH JAZZ**
00843066 .... $16.99

66. **A CHARLIE BROWN CHRISTMAS**
00843067 .... $16.99

67. **CHICK COREA**
00843068 .... $15.95

68. **CHARLES MINGUS**
00843069 .... $16.95

69. **CLASSIC JAZZ**
00843071 .... $15.99

70. **THE DOORS**
00843072 .... $14.95

71. **COLE PORTER CLASSICS**
00843073 .... $14.95

72. **CLASSIC JAZZ BALLADS**
00843074 .... $15.99

73. **JAZZ/BLUES**
00843075 .... $14.95

74. **BEST JAZZ CLASSICS**
00843076 .... $15.99

75. **PAUL DESMOND**
00843077 .... $14.95

76. **BROADWAY JAZZ BALLADS**
00843078 .... $15.99

77. **JAZZ ON BROADWAY**
00843079 .... $15.99

78. **STEELY DAN**
00843070 .... $14.99

79. **MILES DAVIS CLASSICS**
00843081 .... $15.99

80. **JIMI HENDRIX**
00843083 .... $15.99

81. **FRANK SINATRA – CLASSICS**
00843084 .... $15.99

82. **FRANK SINATRA – STANDARDS**
00843085 .... $15.99

83. **ANDREW LLOYD WEBBER**
00843104 .... $14.95

84. **BOSSA NOVA CLASSICS**
00843105 .... $14.95

85. **MOTOWN HITS**
00843109 .... $14.95

86. **BENNY GOODMAN**
00843110 .... $14.95

87. **DIXIELAND**
00843111 .... $14.95

88. **DUKE ELLINGTON FAVORITES**
00843112 .... $14.95

89. **IRVING BERLIN FAVORITES**
00843113 .... $14.95

90. **THELONIOUS MONK CLASSICS**
00841262 .... $16.99

91. **THELONIOUS MONK FAVORITES**
00841263 .... $16.99

92. **LEONARD BERNSTEIN**
00450134 .... $14.99

93. **DISNEY FAVORITES**
00843142 .... $14.99

94. **RAY**
00843143 .... $14.95

95. **JAZZ AT THE LOUNGE**
00843144 .... $14.99

96. **LATIN JAZZ STANDARDS**
00843145 .... $14.99

97. **MAYBE I'M AMAZED**
00843148 .... $14.99

98. **DAVE FRISHBERG**
00843149 .... $15.99

99. **SWINGING STANDARDS**
00843150 .... $14.99

100. **LOUIS ARMSTRONG**
00740423 .... $15.99

101. **BUD POWELL**
00843152 .... $14.99

102. **JAZZ POP**
00843153 .... $14.99

103. **ON GREEN DOLPHIN STREET & OTHER JAZZ CLASSICS**
00843154 .... $14.99

104. **ELTON JOHN**
00843155 .... $14.99

105. **SOULFUL JAZZ**
00843151 .... $14.99

106. **SLO' JAZZ**
00843117 .... $14.99

107. **MOTOWN CLASSICS**
00843116 .... $14.99

111. **COOL CHRISTMAS**
00843162 .... $15.99

Jazz Instruction & Improvisation

Books for All Instruments from Hal Leonard

AN APPROACH TO JAZZ IMPROVISATION

INCLUDES TAB

by Dave Pozzi
Musicians Institute Press

Explore the styles of Charlie Parker, Sonny Rollins, Bud Powell and others with this comprehensive guide to jazz improvisation. Covers: scale choices • chord analysis • phrasing • melodies • harmonic progressions • more.

00695135 Book/CD Pack $17.95

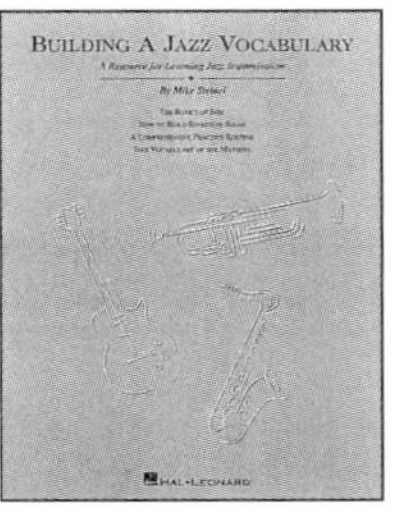

BUILDING A JAZZ VOCABULARY

By Mike Steinel

A valuable resource for learning the basics of jazz from Mike Steinel of the University of North Texas. It covers: the basics of jazz • how to build effective solos • a comprehensive practice routine • and a jazz vocabulary of the masters.

00849911 ....$19.95

THE CYCLE OF FIFTHS

by Emile and Laura De Cosmo

This essential instruction book provides more than 450 exercises, including hundreds of melodic and rhythmic ideas. The book is designed to help improvisors master the cycle of fifths, one of the primary progressions in music. Guaranteed to refine technique, enhance improvisational fluency, and improve sight-reading!

00311114 ....$16.99

THE DIATONIC CYCLE

by Emile and Laura De Cosmo

Renowned jazz educators Emile and Laura De Cosmo provide more than 300 exercises to help improvisors tackle one of music's most common progressions: the diatonic cycle. This book is guaranteed to refine technique, enhance improvisational fluency, and improve sight-reading!

00311115 ....$16.95

EAR TRAINING

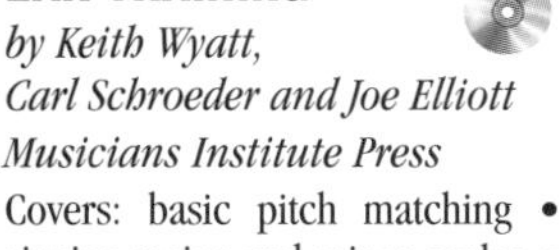

by Keith Wyatt, Carl Schroeder and Joe Elliott
Musicians Institute Press

Covers: basic pitch matching • singing major and minor scales • identifying intervals • transcribing melodies and rhythm • identifying chords and progressions • seventh chords and the blues • modal interchange, chromaticism, modulation • and more.

00695198 Book/2-CD Pack $24.95

EXERCISES AND ETUDES FOR THE JAZZ INSTRUMENTALIST

by J.J. Johnson

Designed as study material and playable by any instrument, these pieces run the gamut of the jazz experience, featuring common and uncommon time signatures and keys, and styles from ballads to funk. They are progressively graded so that both beginners and professionals will be challenged by the demands of this wonderful music.

00842018 Bass Clef Edition $16.95
00842042 Treble Clef Edition $16.95

JAZZOLOGY

The Encyclopedia of Jazz Theory for All Musicians

by Robert Rawlins and Nor Eddine Bahha

This comprehensive resource covers a variety of jazz topics, for beginners and pros of any instrument. The book serves as an encyclopedia for reference, a thorough methodology for the student, and a workbook for the classroom.

00311167 ....$18.95

JAZZ THEORY RESOURCES

by Bert Ligon
Houston Publishing, Inc.

This is a jazz theory text in two volumes. **Volume 1 includes:** review of basic theory • rhythm in jazz performance • triadic generalization • diatonic harmonic progressions and analysis • substitutions and turnarounds • and more. **Volume 2 includes:** modes and modal frameworks • quartal harmony • extended tertian structures and triadic superimposition • pentatonic applications • coloring "outside" the lines and beyond • and more.

00030458 Volume 1 ....$39.95
00030459 Volume 2 ....$29.95

JOY OF IMPROV

by Dave Frank and John Amaral

This book/CD course on improvisation for all instruments and all styles will help players develop monster musical skills! **Book One** imparts a solid basis in technique, rhythm, chord theory, ear training and improv concepts. **Book Two** explores more advanced chord voicings, chord arranging techniques and more challenging blues and melodic lines. The CD can be used as a listening and play-along tool.

00220005 Book 1 – Book/CD Pack $24.95
00220006 Book 2 – Book/CD Pack $24.95

THE PATH TO JAZZ IMPROVISATION

by Emile and Laura De Cosmo

This fascinating jazz instruction book offers an innovative, scholarly approach to the art of improvisation. It includes in-depth analysis and lessons about: cycle of fifths • diatonic cycle • overtone series • pentatonic scale • harmonic and melodic minor scale • polytonal order of keys • blues and bebop scales • modes • and more.

00310904 ....$14.95

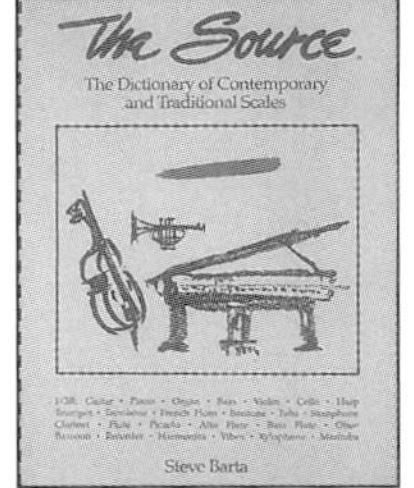

THE SOURCE

The Dictionary of Contemporary and Traditional Scales

by Steve Barta

This book serves as an informative guide for people who are looking for good, solid information regarding scales, chords, and how they work together. It provides right and left hand fingerings for scales, chords, and complete inversions. Includes over 20 different scales, each written in all 12 keys.

00240885 ....$15.95

21 BEBOP EXERCISES

by Steve Rawlins

This book/CD pack is both a warm-up collection and a manual for bebop phrasing. Its tasty and sophisticated exercises will help you develop your proficiency with jazz interpretation. It concentrates on practice in all twelve keys – moving higher by half-step – to help develop dexterity and range. The companion CD includes all of the exercises in 12 keys.

00315341 Book/CD Pack $17.95

THE WOODSHEDDING SOURCE BOOK

by Emile De Cosmo

Rehearsing with this method daily will improve technique, reading ability, rhythmic and harmonic vocabulary, eye/finger coordination, endurance, range, theoretical knowledge, and listening skills – all of which lead to superior improvisational skills.

00842000 C Instruments $19.95

For More Information, See Your Local Music Dealer, Or Write To:

7777 W. Bluemound Rd. P.O. Box 13819 Milwaukee, WI 53213

Visit Hal Leonard online at
www.halleonard.com

Prices, contents & availability subject to change without notice.

0409

The Best-Selling Jazz Book of All Time Is Now Legal!

The Real Books are the most popular jazz books of all time. Since the 1970s, musicians have trusted these volumes to get them through every gig, night after night. The problem is that the books were illegally produced and distributed, without any regard to copyright law, or royalties paid to the composers who created these musical masterpieces.

Hal Leonard is very proud to present the first legitimate and legal editions of these books ever produced. You won't even notice the difference, other than all the notorious errors being fixed: the covers and typeface look the same, the song lists are nearly identical, and the price for our edition is even cheaper than the originals!

Every conscientious musician will appreciate that these books are now produced accurately and ethically, benefitting the songwriters that we owe for some of the greatest tunes of all time!

VOLUME 1
Includes: Autumn Leaves • Body and Soul • Don't Get Around Much Anymore • Falling in Love with Love • Have You Met Miss Jones? • Lullaby of Birdland • Misty • Satin Doll • Stella by Starlight • and hundreds more!

00240221 C Edition $29.99
00240224 B♭ Edition $29.95
00240225 E♭ Edition $29.95
00240226 Bass Clef Edition $29.95
00240292 C Edition 6 x 9 .... $27.95
00451087 C Edition on CD-ROM $25.00

VOLUME 2
Includes: Avalon • Birdland • Come Rain or Come Shine • Fever • Georgia on My Mind • It Might as Well Be Spring • Moonglow • The Nearness of You • On the Sunny Side of the Street • Route 66 • Sentimental Journey • Smoke Gets in Your Eyes • Tangerine • Yardbird Suite • and more!

00240222 C Edition $29.95
00240227 B♭ Edition $29.95
00240228 E♭ Edition $29.95
00240229 Bass Clef Edition $29.95
00240293 C Edition 6 x 9 .... $27.95

VOLUME 3
Includes: Ain't Misbehavin' • Cheek to Cheek • The Lady Is a Tramp • A Nightingale Sang in Berkeley Square • On a Clear Day • Stormy Weather • The Very Thought of You • and more!

00240233 C Edition $29.99
00240284 B♭ Edition $29.95
00240285 E♭ Edition $29.95
00240286 Bass Clef Edition $29.95

Also available:

THE REAL VOCAL BOOK
00240230 Volume 1 High Voice $29.95
00240307 Volume 1 Low Voice $29.99
00240231 Volume 2 High Voice $29.95
00240308 Volume 2 Low Voice $29.95

THE REAL BOOK – STAFF PAPER
00240327 .... $9.95

NOW AVAILABLE: Play-along CDs to some of the most popular songs featured in the world famous *Real Books*. Each volume features selections sorted alphabetically from the 6th edition.

The Real Book Play-Along – Volume 1 A-D
00240302 3-CD Set $24.95

The Real Book Play-Along – Volume 1 E-J
00240303 3-CD Set $24.95

The Real Book Play-Along – Volume 1 L-R
00240304 3-CD Set $24.95

The Real Book Play-Along – Volume 1 S-Z
00240305 3-CD Set $24.95

The Real Book Play-Along – Volume 2 A-D
00240351 3-CD Set $24.99

The Real Book Play-Along – Volume 2 E-I
00240352 3-CD Set $24.99

The Real Book Play-Along – Volume 2 J-R
00240353 3-CD Set $24.99

The Real Book Play-Along – Volume 2 S-Z
00240354 3-CD Set $24.99

FOR MORE INFORMATION, SEE YOUR LOCAL MUSIC DEALER, OR WRITE TO:

7777 W. BLUEMOUND RD. P.O. BOX 13819 MILWAUKEE, WI 53213

Complete song lists online at www.halleonard.com

Prices and availability subject to change without notice.

0210